Pink Instrument

PINK
INSTRUMENT

poems by
MAX BLAGG

photographs by
RALPH GIBSON

LUMEN EDITIONS
A Division of Brookline Books

ISBN: 1-57129-054-0

Library of Congress Cataloging-in-Publication Data

Printed in the United States of America

10 9 8 7 6 5 4 3 2 1

Published by

LUMEN EDITIONS
a division of Brookline Books
P. O. Box 1047
Cambridge, Massachusetts 02238

To order toll-free, call 1-800-666-BOOK

TABLE OF CONTENTS

for Anita

A C K N O W L E D G E M E N T S

Some of these poems were previously published, in slightly
different form, in the chapbooks *From Here to Maternity* (London:
Aloes, 1979; o.p.) and *Licking the Fun Up* (London: Aloes, 1991;
o.p.), for which the author wishes to thank Jim Pennington, and
also the editors of *Bomb, Night, Verbal Abuse, Redtape, Sensible Skin,
A Gathering of the Tribes,* and any other magazines in which these
works have appeared.

Special thanks to Ralph Gibson for his energy and generosity
in this collaboration.

—M. B.

Pink Instrument

FROM HERE TO MATERNITY

Blondes, redheads,
Redheads, blondes
modern girls, smooth but never soft
not butch but two-fisted just in case
wet dreamers slim dancers fast movers slow gliders
"they dance on the springs of the sky"
lip service girls, sisters, solistas of the soir
tiny volcanoes powered by hand
hula dancers cheerleaders barmaids and hitters
slim assassins poised to wreck your life
smiling women who slam the door in your face
after you've spent the rent money on cognac
fleshy envelopes you sleep inside
and forget the address…
Me, I just want a peaceful life, dream interiors,
shiny parquet floors and stainless steel walls
and your heart your bleeding heart
pinned to my designer boudoir floor
so I can step on it each morning on waking,
Squish squish
like a rubber bath mat, squish squish.
And then
there's the kind of woman who
likes to tease the animals
she doesn't mean any harm
she just can't resist
rapping on the bars of the cage
as she strolls by…
and we're on some rooftop
we're on some rooftop
and her skin looks softer
than the silk of my shirt
flesh that photographed like flesh,
you felt you could reach out and touch it
red hair glinting under sodium lights
she is standing on the roof
and the wind is in her hair   3

and I tell her she *is* that woman
and she laughs and glows and goes
I'm tasting fragments of her
perfume on the breeze
as she purrs, she disappears
before my slowly glazing eyes
and you still make promises
that you can never keep
and they will never keep
and they are so damn beautiful
that you want to start all over
but as usual it's too late
to start all over even
though that first moment
when someone you've wanted
someone you have really wanted
gives up her mouth to your mouth
and puts her endless arms around you
and her lips are moving
like animals scenting blood
I know I was too funky for you—
you ditched me because
I used fifteen dollars
of the money I owed you for the pills
on having my stitches taken out
and I forgot to call you
on a Saturday night
when we had a heavy date—
I know I'm not the strong
solvent type.

I have her phone number
on the inside of a match book
I am staring at her phone number
and I will never call her
because I don't know what to say

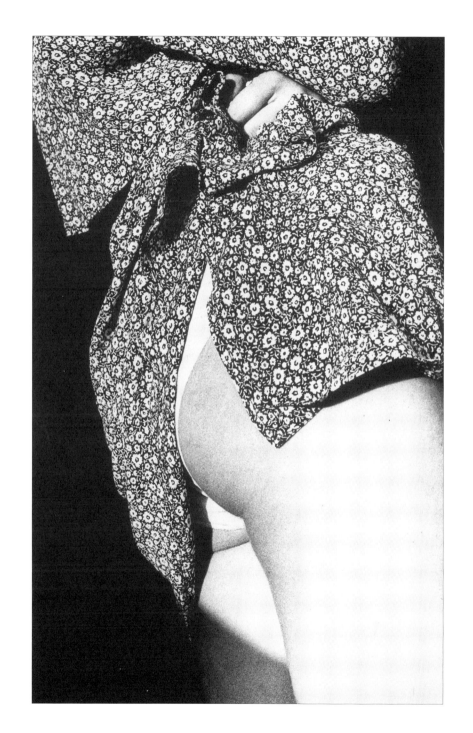

because when I was writing down
the number was the time
when I knew exactly what to say
and now I don't even remember
her face but she was lovely
and she probably still is
but I'm tongue-tied and I feel boring
I feel totally boring
and I have no money again
and how could she possibly understand
that when I say I have no money
I mean I have
no money whatsoever
and I know you will
never understand that
you will never understand that
I don't understand it myself
and I don't care because
when I do have money
When I do have some money
I will send you telegrams and
flowers and other
pointless, expensive gifts
and I won't return your calls
and I'll never sleep with you again
and I know that's no big deal
but it's the best I can do
apart from that it's all
flak and hammer
get in line, get next or go last
it's a jive life a jive life a jive life
a jive life lit by moments of glamour
simplex moments when
life tastes sweet
and the rest is damage.

CARDIAC

I want a car that I can ride in
a power pack cadillac a coked-up cadillac
a rustproof dustproof chrome roof cadillac
a gimcrack cadillac a come-stained cadillac
whacked out cadillac
smokestack cadillac shockstop cadillac
cadillac cadillac lac lac lactose
pure rose cream and shiny
skin tight cadillac fishtit cadillac
switch hit cadillac
fleshtone cadillac shinbone cadillac
assassinated cadillac (that's the JFK
Dallas version of cadillac)
a poontang cadillac! El Dorado! Coup de Ville!
Fleetwood Custom brand new whitewalls
a dismantled cadillac a D-cup cadillac
Jayne Mansfield's head
in the back of her big pink cadillac
and the chihuahuas lying dead on the highway
by the roofless cadillac that bloody caddy
o caddy, o daddy
Cos this ain't no Honda no Buick Skylark,
es no Toyota, no Yamahaha
Forget Ford Fairlane and Chevrolaylay
they ain't our speedo oh no no no no
This is America and we drive cadillacs
cadillacs all kinda cadillacs
Yo, swell fins on this here caddy
Hey flag down that big black caddy
that black black black cadillac
and come on over here
and step inside your daddy's caddy
it's got green leather seats
and folding ashtrays
brand new FM all the options
So we take a drive into the night
and then we park it in the darkness

under a werewolf moon
and come on over here
climb into the back of your daddy's caddy
your slow smile surrounds me
and as you crawl over
that green leather seat
your skirt rides up and I can see
I can see oh say can you see
by that green dashboard light
the sudden flash of shiny thigh
we are coiled like hibernating snakes
in the back of your daddy's caddy
your creamy skin laid on green leather
and isn't that the whitest skin
the whitest skin I've ever seen?
and the radio reminds us
Don't forget the Motor City
oh don't forget the Motor City!
and your left leg is hooked over the front
seat and I've got fluid drive
klik klik your legs are locking
klik klik this caddy's rocking
I can feel the blood beneath
the surface of your seamless skin
I can trace the specific contours
of your skull as surely as
that topographer tracing the contours
of the skin of the planet
and is this not America beneath my hands?
Its mountains and rivers and the missile silos
six miles beneath the cornfields of Kansas?
No, that is not this
this is purely human
stroking you in the back
of your daddy's caddy
stoking you in the back
of your daddy's caddy
Listen to my blood humming
listen to my heart coming

and the tumblers fall into place
and the padlock pops and
you slide wide open
and we're wrapped in
this perfect envelope of flesh
in the back of your daddy's caddy
and your private parts are more perfect
than the grillwork on an El Dorado
O caddy, o daddy!
O sweet god of motor cars
there is no cadillac
Cadillac is just one of the
alltime great American words
and I wish I wish I wish—
I wish your daddy was here to see it.

Get Well Soon

Thanks for the note it says
Blue skies/nothing but blue skies/ from now on
It's a mistake to fall in love with memories
and I've abandoned the concept of
woman as a romantic goddess
That's a barefaced lie but still—
He fell in love she was terrific
But that winter the sky changed
and her mind seemed to change
from moment to moment
always in some state of artificial distress
funny you really don't look that distressed
but then, why should you?
It's my problem right? It's my problem
please I insist you must have the last word
you're always in the right
you're the original Miss Right—
don't slam the door on your way out—
but I don't want to spend the rest of my life
in search of mental health
or mystic mammals or mummies or mantras
or Miss Universe or Miss Subways…
When I said I'd never let you go
I actually meant it
Did you think I was just
some theatrical queen
you demented little freak?
I should have clocked it then,
you'd always let me down.
Ever watch eels after
their heads are cut off
continue to reel like eels?
and this warped vision
of *woman* and *my woman*
and *Hey she's my woman!*
don't you look at my woman!
Look up at the sun it shines down on you

without mercy or special dispensation
Sure and it's just the little pains of life
just life and only just
you see I know it's like that,
it's not your fault it's just New York
the way it turns everything
to fever and nightmare
and that's just the way you like it!
Blue skies, nothing but blue skies
looking for blue skies, sky's all gone.

Another Friday night or Monday night,
not special and you're not special,
and neither is the way you handle it
Hey amoré startles you doesn't it and
tenderness and the slow velvet strokes
of the spokes of the wheel of love,
the hand of friendship in the night
well if you can kick it, I can kick it too
I got solid shoes now, I'm
steeltipped and tightlipped
and if anybody looks at me wrong
I'll break their muthafuckin' jaw
but I hate to be this way
because I know I know
How can anyone have a normal life in New York?
well nobody can, that's why we're here,
but we all adapt somehow,
so why push it, why push it
out the window of the 33rd floor
and you're sorry you say you are so sorry
and last night was the worst night
the longest night of my life
and you weren't there
and I don't want you to be sorry
Please, you say, please, I'm just a little tease
I wasn't your main squeeze I was just joking
well I'm choking, choking on it
I'm gonna choke it up

and you can choose your bandage
yeah you're a tease and while
you blow the leading man
I'm nothing more than your
halfwit gimmick assistant
so pass me that spanner or
some sharp object
a bludgeon a hammer a gun
gimme a blade a propeller
gimme an outboard motor
gimme ticket for an aeroplane
and let me fly away
you made me ugly, I didn't wanna do it,
I didn't want to do it
but I agree to be disgraceful now
and I can see your shaved head from here
You're just a mannequin
your expression never changes
Your rubber words bounce off my leather jacket
and I'm standing here holding a hologram.

Over the telephone your indignant soprano
is moving but essentially plastic
So pass that potion let me rub that lotion
in to those leatherette boots
they're just like your fake passions
and your blue skies
There aren't any blue skies
don't look for blue skies sky's all gone
and sure I can swell up and
call up a sex object
but do you think that's what I wanted
is that what I wanted?
I put gloves on my nerves
and teeth in my mouth and head on out—
out of doors out to lunch totally out of it
screaming to a halt on the street
when somebody looks like you
performing my autistic gymnastics

in a shitstorm of torn blue notes
like goons slutting in the enormous
midriff of summer
What was it then? What was it worth
because it don't mean a thing
if it ain't got that hinge
it's just another moonlight mile
or the ghost of a smile
or a nail driven through your palm
and then I pull you down
I pull you down to my level
Hello angel!
You no longer steam up
my thought reports each
blank day unfolds without you
curved into the shape of the morning
and in my nose the stink of city life
fierce and freakish it saves me somehow
so cancel that last dance
you had your last chance
I'm back to normal New York
and I feel sick sick sick
I'm gonna vomit whoah I threw up
on your red dress and
your hi-heel sneakers
what a mess I made
and I always blame myself
so why don't you take it to the cleaners,
you take it to the cleaners
and bleach out every last
trace of your bullshit
don't ask me for blue skies
there are none.

And don't you find that having to be
someone you aren't
can be a strain sometimes?
This is all just romantic fallout
I cancel the airstrike on your loft

and awake in the ruins of my own
calm as a triple beam of sunlight
I screw in my eye and strap on my hook
it's shiny steel and I sing a solo
I don't want you I don't need you
I don't love you anymore
and I limp out the door
your face is distant fading fast
nothing, nothing lasts
how easy it all seemed
those magic moments
tripping light fantastic and you
were solid perfect incapable of harm
everything was promised and
nothing delivered I cut my way out
of this belladonna marcella
fellini whistlin' dixie
hambone rising in a blue mist delusion
I want you to kneel
like a doggie in the dark
while I glatter and pummel
the perfect globes of
your snow white ass until
they glow like the midnight special
and shine shine shine
their everlovin' light on me,
until they're as red as my eyes
instead I simply kneel and I say
pray for small mercies
and small mercies might pray for you.

Licking the Fun Up

"To begin to begin again/turning the inside out"
—*W. C. Williams*

Advice from the good doctor on how
to survive in this Babylon
this "garden of longing
sown with the seeds of ruin"
this unrequited howling for more
more of everything, of anything
we tell lies, invent new lives
conjure up a lifestyle that fits right in
with the movies and TV
play happy and sad and brutalized
all at once for the sake of realism.
It's a perfect October day
the kind that sets your hair on fire
children dancing in a leaf storm
along St. Luke's Place
a brilliant blue sky showing
the pink edge of winter
the turning of the year and the heart
and the yearnings of the heart
a time when dying seems impossibly far off
when the light caresses each
single brick in the wall it hits.
The sun hits the wall
and you want to be part of that
part brick part wall part sunlight
and you feel as fragile as Humpty Dumpty
and you think of children and
living and trying to go on
but the sky changes and the season changes
And now you decline as gracefully as you can
the offers of the beggars and the
window washers who fill the streets
and the heat that pours down like liquid Drano
from a sky the color of a rotten peach

ignore the mayhem reported
daily on the so called news
terminal cases in body bags
sacks of meat heading for the morgue
essential fluids seeping into the linoleum
of fifth floor walk-ups and welfare hotels
distant horrors in other boroughs
chubby losers wearing wires
to snare their brothers
politicians committing suicide
in their suburban kitchens
secretaries abducted from shopping malls
who later turn up dead in heavily wooded areas
and their cars traced to a motel in Florida
where the suspect takes the Fifth
or the Carmen Miranda
you have the right to remain silent
and since you did it
you might as well remain silent
all these dreary stories relayed to you
by failed comedians and amateur actors
who can barely read a teleprompter
it makes you so weary
nothing but blood and heat
and guns and dying
you need gloves for your nerves
just to walk out the door.
So why worry about the dollar
plunging like a diver,
like a hawk on a vole, plunging to earth,
no, not like a hawk
a hawk has elegance, beauty, dignity,
it has a purpose and a need, a reality
that the Dow Jones pork belly
futures will never have
and I wish I could figure the difference
between our magazine lives
and the life of a hawk or the difference
between a hawk and a handgun

we're neckdeep in a world of plastic
it's a sinking feeling, a Poland state of mind
for thirty seconds you're necking
with Marilyn Monroe in Dansk
and for the next eight hours
they're stomping your kidneys in Krakow
and can somebody please throw in the towel
and you've spit out your mouthpiece
and you're crawling to a neutral corner
and your face looks like
Isabella Rossellini in *Blue Velvet*
all that raw pulpy flesh, blue bruises
and where is that bright manimal boy
who was once running to tie your shoe,
a Molotov cocktail in his spare hand?
and daddy the fun's gone
all of the fun gone.

For years you let yourself
be stroked and pampered
the way someone might pamper
a lovely but brainless pet.
But now you don't spend much
time in the mirror anymore
you're growing ragged around the edges,
mangy, your hair falling out,
your entire corpus in total disrepair
and those who stroked you then
are in the market for a shotgun today
and you can understand that
but still you want to get back
you want to be pure again
mend the shredded nets
of your spirit catcher
absolve yourself somehow
of all the medical waste
you've snorted and smoked
and eaten and otherwise
crammed into the shaky vessel

that carries you around
the wheezing envelope of flesh
that totters daily closer to the edge.
Baby, baby, where did the fun go
where did the fun go?
It all happened so fast
one minute you were sliding
on greased lightning
moving right along
grinning blindly into the camera
then suddenly, suddenly
you ground to a halt
you were ground up in tiny particles
and laid along a mirror
and when the mirror was empty
you licked the snot from her nose
and then you drank her piss
pretending to impress her
with your Aztec priest routines
but really to get high from the residue
Yes you were a haiku man in those days
you liked it short and tight
and now years later you
flip through your kodachromes
trying to figure out
which sullen beauty put her disease in you
It's too late to be pure
you're swaying slightly now and praying
a man on his knees
in front of some terrible news
and you want to get a handle on it
because you can't handle it
you never learned you didn't try
you gave up on the second lesson
you weren't interested you didn't care
you forgot about it canned it
blinked and looked away
looked and moved on
you underestimated

the shelf life of a sex maniac
and when things got tough
you whined and lay down
like some sick barnyard animal
you are one skinned monkey
and you stop no show
your aura disappeared
along with your memory
down those raw dawn streets
you couldn't even recall
that her eyes were blue
and how they moved you
you careened off the page
dead or drunk or both
the needle went right off the meter
on your bullshit detector
you were totally bogus
defective in every way
and it's going to take more
than simple faith
to return from this sorry state.
Your anti-damage systems are rusted out
the chrome is off your bumper Jack
and a three coat paint job
is not going to cover the scars
in your body armor
you are sucking the fumes up
sucking the fumes up
and daddy the fun's gone
all of the fun gone
and the well run dry.

It is time to call a halt
to your imbecilic acquiescence!
Don't be led into temptation just say no
you've read it on your shopping bag
just say no
you've seen it on the telly, just say no,
so much to turn down

in these Babylonian times…
Say no to thin lips and stock tips
say no to infiltrators and oil change experts
short change specialists and lube job jockeys
extending their thin fingers
into your inside pocket
Say no to walking the dog while
the postman checks your wife's mail
Say no to moussaka in the Socrates coffee shop
When a handsome young man in a black chiffon
dress asks for the next dance say no
Don't just say yes because
it rhymes with dress say no!
Say no to living according to
the dictates of your horoscope
say no to the strange chamber of Venus
if you're not packing rubber
say no to scientology roy rollogy
and all the other ologies
say no to alligator appetizers in Cajun joints
say no to porcupine stew when
you're passing through the Ivory Coast
say no to sun dried tomatoes
from Dean and Delirious at 22 clams a kilo
sometimes a tomato is just a tomato
Say no to chinese food for breakfast
and vodka for lunch same day say no
Let your kidneys do the talking say no!
Say no to Texaco Pennzoil and United
Airlines doing what they do best
Say no to Tokyo as the yen takes hold
say no to jacking another
round into the chamber and killing
your girlfriend because she's fourteen and
pregnant and you don't have a job
but you do have a .38 special
Say no to bible thumpers
pounding on hookers in motel rooms
Say no to old macaroni and cheese

and all the other aging food
growing wings in your fridge say no
Say no to the dry cleaner
who lost your best pants
when he asks if a twenty will cover it
say no to jive lawyers and landlords
with their teeth in your throat
Say no to the distaff and
Falstaff and the general staff
say no to the nipple of any liquor
bottle winking on your shelf
say no to burying your head in books
while the days run away
Say no to putting your mind out to pasture
say no to riding the roundabout
when the swings aren't even loaded
and swinging the lead
when you could be pumping iron
say no to fake sweats fainting fits
and other Victorian deliriums
say no to sudden reversals
shunting of the facts
say no to my ugliness laid out before you
Say no to this and this and this:
If it's pissing rain or raining piss
what's the difference in a choke hold?
Whether they've got you by the throat
or by the balls they've got you
and the only way to let it go is to say so
No thank you, no way, no how, no go
No and No and No!

The simple ways of the Masai,
drinking bull's blood, hunting lion with a spear
copulating with nubile maidens
how peaceful they seem
in contrast to your nickel and dime problems
and the solutions offered by
your very close friends;

your throat is raw from screaming
and they suggest a low tar cigarette
Your eyes bleed and they give you
the name of some cut rate optician
your head falls off
and they pass you the crazy glue
your sperm count drops to
three over two hundred
and they advise you
to substitute egg whites
your heart stops
and they hand you a metronome…
You just can't seem to put your
shoulder to the wheel
you can't fill it to the rim, Jim.
The school of humming
dancing and jacking it around
is closed for the season
and you're left holding an emery board
and three chipped nails
you're about as smart as a bag of hammers
somebody licked all the fun up
while your back was turned
you are one stunned white man
looking for a way back in
and the future might not be there
when you arrive!

The firestorm is about to commence
the shittra is about to hit the fan
the blowtorch is about to be
applied to the testicles
the electrodes are right now
being clipped to the nipples
the nicotine fit is on
the junkies are being cut off at the source
the American army is burning the coca fields
and all your friends' noses
have been surgically blocked.   27

Anyone owning a pet must report
immediately to the Destruction Center
It's a tough time for everyone
the yen is way up and the dollar is way down
the locals are turning on the tourists
and your gold card won't buy
a toilet roll in this town
The shutters slam down
in the market place at your approach
The milk is rotten the meat is rank
and the riverboat is not due for 48 hours.
So then you might take a train
yes you might ride the rails
a fast train a train that will carry you
to many distant cities
steel wheels rocking through the rain
loading up on iron music
lullabies and sexsongs
something real something
you can bite down on
the Santa Fe Zephyr the Midnight Special
shine its everlovin' light on you
American trains or
steel wheels clicking all the way
to the Gothic stations of old Europa
Trans Europe express gleaming
in the halls of Rotterdam
Barcelona Milano Zaragoza
or a freight train out of Dresden
during a bombing raid
B-29's droning low overhead
and those thousand pounders
they rock the earth around you
now that is heavy metal
and if you survive it
the names of the stations alone will soothe you
tone your shrieking down
to something smoother on the ear
and the Eiffel Tower can do

wonders for your sex life too,
if you happen to be passing through Paris
when you arrive at the Gare Du Nord
look up into the electric light
and you might see Paul Eluard
swinging from the bars
and he's chanting this chanson
"I sing the great joy of singing you
of having you or not having you"
and you feel like you understand
where he's coming from
because when you walk under the erectile mass
the vertical girders do resemble exactly
a pair of enormous immaculate thighs
hiked up above a tiny French dress
and gleaming like they should
oiled and supple but jesus are they firm
yeah verily they are steely dan, steely mantraps
ready to lick up the fun with anyone
whose motor's jumping
like the pump on the heart, pumping.

Or you may find yourself
at the edge of some land
you are glad to be standing on
dawn coming up and a
fierce rhythm fills your sails
the hammered steel lure
flashes in the light
as it arches out into the rip
where the fish are feeding
the hook takes hold
and when the struggle is over
and the creature lies glistening at your feet
it is "as lovely a thing as the gods have made"
fish are simple creatures
their hearts have only two chambers,
flaky derringers in a submarine world
but they are beautiful in their ferocity

in their tenacity of life
you turn the fish back in to the ocean
and return to face the fact that
this is a man's world and you are under it
down there where the fish are
but you lack their elegant apparatus
you need to breathe,
breathe in and breathe out
suck up the tiny pockets of air
drift slowly to the surface
where the sky waits, pure azure
aching with promise
grip the skyhook and ride it
across a heaven of your own imagining
where the air tastes like atomized clearasil
sharp brilliant colors explode behind the eyes
everything as crisp as a poppadum
a new treasury bill
watch the full moon rising through mist
as the afternoon fades
a flight of geese preceding it
making a Japanese poem.

You've reached the end of the road of excess
and the palace of wisdom
has long since been demolished
but the ocean's pre-Cambrian rhythms
will hose you down
if you really do want to be pure
If you want to be something more
than a punch drunk liverwhipper
whose bed sheets reek of the toxin
leaking from your valves.
Your sweat was once a famous aphrodisiac
and now you stink
like any other chemical plant
your poisons seeping
into the general pollution
alarming shoppers in the pharmacy

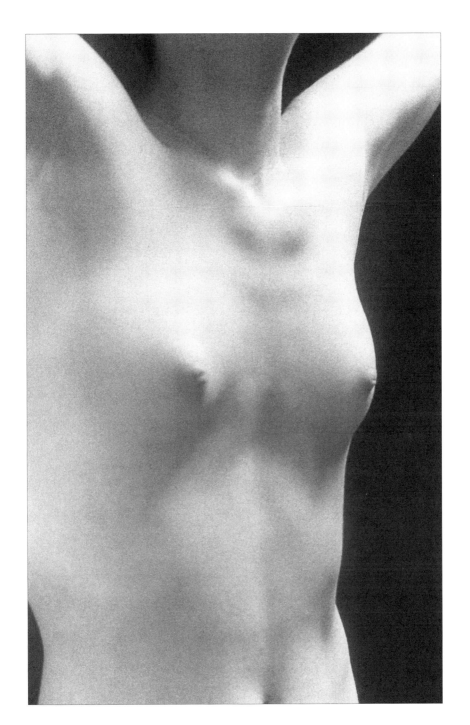

where you've gone looking
for some ozone busting deodorant
to cut the rank impurity…
O daddy you are in terrible shape
so shake it, kick it, kick that habit
put all your tired shit in the shredder
take up a fighting stance against the moon
and all those retrograde planets
that are turning your mind
to mush and maggot food.

You need some rhythm to carry you back
or punt you onward
a spherical melody that will click in the brain
some cluster of sounds a sequence a plan
a man a plan a Canal, Panama
a voice in the wilderness
humming a brand new tune
a modern sound banging like a gong
because you must go on
you must study the intricate
threads of a spider's web
inhale the formal odor of a rosebush
polish the shiny lanterns of a new red rover
beaming signals to Jupiter
jump to the subcutaneous
bebop of slangy tramps
observe the motion of the snowy bat
steering by radar
toward a clotted mass of insects
back to the lab Doctor, back to the lab
the gloss cracking on the china
the way your picture window shatters
into new patterns
into a roadmap you can follow
on fleet feet and fresh tunes
spring loaded
they go in deeper than a gravity knife
spearing the ears of innocent bystanders

as your red wagon blitzes along the highway
spraying a hot load of raw music
luscious rivers of sound
that tear a hole in the oncoming traffic
and send campers careening
over cliffs in your wake
a sensual combination of
rending metal and burning gasoline
filling your eager nostrils
your drummer hooks into thunder
and cooks up a gravity storm
that tears the mind from its mooring
and you are bent into shape
or at least a better shape
than the shape you are in
power spasms jolting the sleepy beast
semi-conductors pouring on the overload
pure electricity swelling the cables
till a godless bloody howling fills the air
and in the studio of broken records
we discover you on all fours
barking into the mike
like a doberman recovering from a coronary
one Babylonian under a groove at last
you blast into the top five!
and this is what you're saying
sometimes I feel like I've got it,
like honey on the tongue
once in a great while I achieve
this state of loony grace
the space between
thinking and breathing
between jumping and falling
the split second before impact
when I'm launched, I'm out there
and it's too good not to share,
because I can't sing
I can't dance I can't paint
but I get this need

I want to put the Word
in your ear
It's a deep thrill
like sex, or mescaline
or sex and mescaline
and then it's gone in a minute
and I don't believe it really happened
but it did happen, it happened to me
and when it does I can transcend
the hum hum drumming
of my ordinary life
I can rise above this body in the chair
and I feel tight tight
every muscle is tight
there is not one ounce of
surplus fat on my body
and that O-negative blood
is pounding through clean veins
and I stomp down Broadway
with my hair on fire
like the Vikings who
ran screaming into battle
with their hair in flames
and I am feeling directly connected
hot wired to language
and words curving into ecstatic shapes
striding down Broadway
sparks jumping from my head
lit up from the inside
glowing in the dark
planning on telling anyone
who crosses my path
about the light in my head
and the light in the street
turning granite into gold
making New York look so embraceable
sexy fierce lines of this curveless city
architecture and geometry turning me on.
The problem is that such moments are rare indeed

most times when I'm walking down Broadway
I'm just walking down Broadway
secretaries and receptionists
dentists and file clerks
may well be subject to the same delusions
and if they too sometimes dream
of magnetic blondes bouncing
on celestial trampolines
then I salute them
because there's no greater thrill
when the flakes fall away
and I get a grip on the tedium
squeeze my grief into a shape I can handle
and sink back into the buttery caress
of the word and the flesh.

PIRANHA LOGIC

"But who is this? What thing of sea or land
that comes this way sailing
Like some stately ship of Tarsus
bound for the Isles of Javan or Gadire…"
Or was it St. Mark's Place or was she
crossing Canal Street in that late
November sunlight when
my heart stopped on the crosswalk
as this vision derailed me
and I wanted to assume
the position and kneel
crawl between the space
of the instep and the heel
of her Maud Frizon shoe
like I wanted to jump into the
ashtray when a shotgun pointed
its enormous muzzle
at the skinny traverse of my chest
a different kind of shrinkage
But this, this, it expands the physical
Who? What? Where? I'm hit
I'm struck by the utter loveliness
of this creature bathed in light
and she is tuned just about fine
she is wrapped real tight
her program is all in order
she has the green light she
is all systems a go-go and
Bang! I go off like biphetamine
popping in the throat
my butcher's hook swings haywire
as she purrs across the traffic
I madly kickstart my motor in
hot pursuit of the prime of my life
her moves as pure as a hawk
riding the thermals and just as distant
and by the time I do get on she's long gone,

she's in the wind
and by some miracle I am not
crushed by a Macktruck
I reach the sidewalk and lean my face
against the phone booth
victim of a massive stroke
of luck at even seeing this being
and being alive on the same street
she fleets along on feet
that I would fit firmly in my mouth
in pure pedal ecstasy…
what an easy mark I am but I don't care
Who was that? Was that you?
Yoo hoo! Hello sailor!
You shook me you ripped me off my rock
and turned me inside out like an octopus
I love your style and
"I love the way you walk/
Boom boom boom boom!"
and my imagination conjures
endless configurations
of the splendors of your flesh
you own that flesh, and
on that flesh you wear a dress!
And is this really the way I talk
you find that hard to believe
And so you leave…
and there you go and you
and you and you
all you lovely women,
walking away
But still you occupy a like space
you breathe the same air
how fortunate this piranha
to have simply been there!

GATHERING BRUISES

for Cookie

October light triggers an avalanche of sighs
each sunset full of small regrets
this thin world stripped
of another spiritcatcher
luminous creature whose
tattooed hands and silver rings
lit up the rat race whose
feral eyes spelled danger
despite her great sweet heart
shaman's gaze cracking the lens
in some long gone New York night
as she leans against the doorjamb
a deep blonde illuminated
from the inside out and if you look
into her eyes they are green green
green she glows in the dark
So now I'm dreaming of the past
I am conjuring you Cookie as you
step from a cab into the pouring rain
with that diamond smile
and your golden hair piled high
who could ever say "No" to you?
we all spread our raincoats in the mud
and guided you inside you
knew where you were going
it was 1979 or thereabouts
everybody had a tiny purse
and a massive appetite
and we were gunning it
no navigator no mercy
wired to the sky kicking
the doors off their hinges and
dancing with broken bottles
biting down hard on

anything that moved
there were some gorgeous moments
and everybody and you looked
like you would live forever.

I Am For You

I am for your long long jacaranda hands
kneading focaccia bread on a Sunday
in the South of August
I am for the primeval and not for the prim
I am for seizures of holy writ and
mad gaskets flailing away
I am for expensive garments that drape correctly
I am for sinuousness but not for sin
I am for snow in winter
and cotton under the sun
I am for oiled bodies scattered on beaches
opalescent creatures stretched on blankets
like the spokes of a heavenly wheel
I am for winding all these strands
into a rhythm that will pulse in time
to the quick motor of the blood
flowing surely in our veins
a silken rope that binds the days
into an endless chain of memory and desire
I am for the green hills of Tuscany
seen through a winescreen
and twirling you around the
dance floor in Italian hill towns
and a bottle or two, no more,
of that vernacchia with
the golden glint, the shiny patina
I am for your gossamer mouth
and threading tall tales
into your ear and I am for your ears
and the tiny points of light
balanced on them under a brand new moon
my silver turning slowly over my heart in place
and the singing stars at night
and strolling on the beach at dawn
as bonita leap in silvery arcs
of chrome-colored light,

feeding my exuberance,
and standing still and breathing
breathing in, breathing out,
I am for that.

The Bump

Walking out of the pharmacy
I felt the bones in my daughter's hand,
fragile as a birds'
as that small owl dead on the road
by Chip's Garage
I took him home for a decent burial
and after asking permission
from the Lord of the Birds
to keep his beautiful feet
with their fishhook talons
and delicate feathering
hoping he would not need them
in his next incarnation
I lopped them off with a sharp axe
and laid him to rest
in that corner of the backyard
where the evening light falls
like grace on the goldenrod
Blake's footprint on
the stretching field
a possibility of deliverance
hovering in the creamy
oxygen of the air
her hand is in my hand and
the delicacy of her skeletal structure
is marvelous and terrifying
she has put murder in me
this tiny thing this Ming vase
and I want to be butch
I wanna be a steeltipped, asskicking,
bodybagging daddy-o
a dada longlegs a true surrealista
a hardbodied padre who
will clear a path for her
through the encroaching ruins
put the deep boot into any jackal's ribs
who comes sniffing round

our campfire without a permit
protect her with beauty truth
and maximum firepower
against all the animals
abroad in America
the impending contact
and impact of this tabloid world
the vulgar metal slamming of cars and
guns vibrating even at the edge
of this last gold day of September,
as the rude boys rock the fences
in the playground on Thompson Street
the angle of the light already changed
as it streams through the gaps in the tenements
and the sun slides down toward December.

I could always get a gun but
when I had the nine millimeter
X. gave me for safekeeping
I never knew where to keep it
I didn't even know how to cock it
properly always wondering if
I'd left one in the chamber
when I took out the clip
half expecting it go off without warning
like an alarm clock or a bomb
popped the hammer once by accident
when I was showing it off to someone
it clicked on empty but
it could have taken out a big chunk
of your beautiful mahogany bookcase
I laughed it off but felt really stupid
because it was obvious I didn't have a handle
on the the basic mechanics of an automatic
finally gave it to a mutual friend who claimed
the owner owed him money
he said he would get me a revolver
to replace it but so far he hasn't.

ACROSS 14TH STREET

Twenty years ago the wind
took my hat down this street
as I stumbled home from Max's
one stunned monkey one shrunk pumpkin
one "dilapidated diseuse"
without carkey or cabfare
unable to make the meat connection
I staggered home starving
for food and affection
east toward the river and the wind
blowing me and my hat down 14th street
toward those red white and blue smokestacks
across the DMZ to where I lived
between Fear and Trembling
the last few blocks I would try
to make the enemy think I was tooled up
by conspicuously holding my pocket
but it was only my head that was loaded.

A silken rag removes that last
thin particle of dyspepsia
hanging from my chin
mad about nothing
and angry at everything
I'm just a swollen bag of rage sometimes
beneath this thin bohemian veneer
this sweet suit I mooched last year
pockets always inside out
feed me clothe me gimme free drinky
it's the twelfth child syndrome
"I didn't earn it but I deserve it anyway"
and when I don't get it
you might find me quivering in a corner
ready to smash windows and faces
of the places and the people I claim to love
homicidal menopausing stickpin
a step away from the Tombs or

that man in rags sitting at
the junction of Union Square
"I could be you, ugly fucker,"
I think to myself as
I drop a quarter into his claw
and peer down the bland
expanse of lower Fourth
the row of bookstores long gone
their bumpy wooden floors
and moody clerks
nervously eyeing the speedfreaks
jetting around the shelves
all that knowledge dispersed
into libraries and dumpsters
gum drying and spines cracking
in pristine first editions
I too am merging with history
slightly foxed, a few pages missing
disappearing like those scruffy bookmen
but still vaguely self-conscious
of being a man wheeling a stroller
into the future along 14th street
A queen of my acquaintance
is walking west we
haven't met in a year at least
and yet we scarcely pause
in our perambulations
"Is that yours?" he says,
feigning interest in the breeder lifestyle
"If not mine, whose?"
I reply enigmatically
we part with meager smiles
pasted to prim lips
dimly recalling our singular versions
of the larks we once pipped
and nothing is delivered
uncovered revived
our gossip and our grief intact.

2ND AVENUE

Benedetta Barzini never slept
with Gerard Malanga
and she's still furious
he faked the whole romance
all those love poems totally bogus
he always did set off my bullshit detector
but he looked utterly glamorous
getting into a cab at St. Mark's Place
on my third day here
in this bulging tent of a city
somebody I recognized
even if it was from a Warhol movie
and the first party I went to
there was Brigid Polk
wearing the same greasy turtleneck
she wore in *Chelsea Girls*
it was just like the movie
a movie about the movie
it all merged like day and night merged
walking down Second Avenue
past the holy house of St. Mark's
church of my heart church of the word
cockeyed spire pointing to
fierce American skies
crammed with poets and poems
that filled my head and blended into
the sweet smell of gasoline
the iron roar of Second Avenue traffic
whirling pell-mell downtown
metallic symphony of cars
and cabs and trucks injecting
pedestrians with that click–click
speed city rhythm
that urban throb
truckloads of food and furniture
shunting and bouncing
over the potholes

Chinese Burmese Indian
restaurants passing in a blur
of hieroglyphic neon
Cheap Jack's and Ratner's and
Schacht's smoked fish
and the bodies cooling in
the funeral parlor at Third
Street close by Tony's café deluxe
where we began each day
guzzling scrambled eggs off the formica
with the hardcore mulatto
ghost ship sailors the chocolate
skinned ambulance dancers
I had the fever for their
brown-eyed handsomeness
they only loved girls and
I wanted to change that
I wanted to crack them like walnuts
bevel their edges
reshape their priorities
but they laughed in my face
when I tried to get sexy
they were nice so nice
tall dark anacondas
sipping homemade daiquiris
words flying like sparks
as they cracked the dexy whip
left me tongue tied and french fried
dried out drier than Betty Ford
"I let the air outa your sangwich baby"
I tried to emulate their diamond style
with the hot white wire of methedrine
hoping my goofball stare
might somehow shatter hearts
when I tottered into bars
on those 8th Street platform heels
doubling my sense of elevation
looking for much more than a simple kiss
my arm holding a fist

and demanding a leg a jambon
the whole ham dripping grease and cracklins
lunch was always turning into dinner
my medulla full of darts and
thorns and dirty deeds not dreamed
but done in daylight and moonlight
in doorways and hallways
pool rooms and rent parties
broken locks and standup cocks
popping like mushrooms
blurred snapshots of a goon world
extreme conditions documented
in the flare of a flash bulb
polaroids fanned like cards in a giddy fist
my faux Borsalino still
balanced on my head
at the most potent moments
the shutter clicked
but the hammer never came
all the way down
and "I love this stinking town"
New York the everturning wheel
that grinds exceeding fine.

FEDERAL DAYS

October November
lightning and sunsets
season of well documented mists
the solid map of streets and the steel web
of the bridge behind them
I call these federal days
the ones that bathe in this specific light
autumn in its plenitude
the juicy flesh of swollen apples
brought to an edible gleam
by simply rubbing them on my sleeve
they begin to shine
like the almost imperceptible swelling
in the cricketer's soft cream flannel pant
when an old leather ball is rubbed against it,
seam to inseam on a green field far away.

NITROUS

Another good Friday opens its golden throat
a harpoonload of honey-colored light
arching over Brooklyn
in 23 years I hardly ever went to Brooklyn
and if I did have to go there
I was always happy to get back across the bridge
to streets with numbers
the clear delineation of uptown and downtown
to the women who remind me of Mona Bump
her drive her drivel her swivel hips
illuminating a side street in a coalmining town
somewhere in Yorkshire
or the streets of Rome
or seen from a crosstown bus as she navigates
the Spanish stores along 14th
her bilingual curves
assassinate the senses
an overload of rich nutritious booty
on the way somewhere
somewhere exciting and I'm not invited
I say *hey Mona.*
hey hey hey Mona
even the drunks on the sidewalk stir
at this articulation of the sacred
cocks rise feebly from their drowning pool
swelling the ropy pipe into
the vague approximation of a fighting stance
but Mona has already moved on
she is ubiquitous
like the nitrous my dentist feeds me
as he does my bridgework
he's Nicaraguan and he understands poets
he knows they need a heavy dose of gas
and a special payment schedule
he cranks the hose
and I am immediately connected
to a sequence of extravagant, grandiose,

hilarious notions which go careening off down
vast corridors in twenty seven different
directions at hundreds of miles an hour
the nerves in my jaw vibrate faintly
like catgut strummed inside a wet towel
distant as a door slammed
in a house on the next block
a welter of glyphs and cyphers
brilliant unutterable remarks
ricochet around the cranium
a solid tumbling declension
of lock and interlock
moving smooth as a projectile
fired from a cannon
booming and zooming
through a milky stratosphere
a sword passing through silk
feathery cloud formations
breathing in soft exhalations
ecstatic milliseconds preceding
a sudden rubbery exit
into the overhead light
the spittoon swirling
bloody water
into a naughahyde void
my last words
"More gas, Mona, more gas!"

MURDER

Each time I cross Houston Street
I touch my collar
with a reverence not entirely faked
the place where two roads intersect
carries powerful magic
criminals were hanged on the gallows here
and the choice of four paths
bewildered the departing spirits
left them stranded
and pissed off at everybody…
on my third day in New York
I had just loaded an old Pentax
so I could send home some tourist snaps
to prove I really was in New York
that there were real bums
on the Bowery
that there really was a Bowery
when suddenly at Houston street
a man lay dead beneath a sheet,
real blood leaked into the gutter
panic ventilated the air
some people shouting and
others calmly walking by
continuing on their daily rounds
as a body lay on the pavement by their feet
I started to take pictures
but it was just too personal
and I walked away from
the mystery beneath the sheet.

In the weeks that followed a sequence
of violent public events
constantly reminded me
I no longer lived in Hampstead
someone threw a table from the window
of a transient hotel on Bleecker Street
it landed on a passerby and

flattened him into the sidewalk
I saw the photo on the front page
of the *Daily News* a white sheet
with a fedora placed on top of it
the sheet looked terribly familiar
and there was something under it
that had once been a man
walking, wearing a hat thinking
about the rent or the Yankees
when death in the form of
a flying table came to claim him
another month passed
I was running across Houston
late for an interview about
a busboy situation
a cop car zoomed past siren wailing
and turned left onto Bowery
thirty seconds later it came
peeling back around the corner
and drew level with me on the sidewalk
the door swung open and
the cop in the passenger seat
was pointing his revolver at my chest.
Everything got quiet
an enormous silence waiting to be filled
by the simple click of a hammer
is my last breath floating somewhere
in this New York air?
Any sudden movement
might put me under a sheet
quick as that dead man
a few weeks before
the cop said pull your coat back real slow
I used my thumb and forefinger to carefully
open my coat and peel it
away from my body
gazing into the void contained
within the steel circle of the barrel
my death hovering there

ready to shed its full metal jacket
and come tearing into the tender flesh
I was wearing suspenders maybe
he had seen a silver glint from them
he didn't say just abruptly
slammed the door and roared off
leaving me holding my lapels
as wide as Houston Street
lights changing
traffic moving along
and my knees beginning to tremble
at the possibilities of
impact, tissue damage,
hospitals, bloody white sheets
imbeciles in blue
trigger-happy puppets
holding my life
in their hairy knuckled hands
down by the crossroads.

Spring Load

When spring comes
the flowers leap out of earth
with the power of dancers
straining for the sun
summoned from their
subterranean habitat
by the vibrations of the light
bursting from their kernels
their cosy kennels
up through cold earth
up into the air
the blue air connected
to my blue heaven
it is the hammer of the sun
that drives them on
and they take their places one
by one in the sweet gush of spring
I finger the dark soil
and turn it in my hands
pull a branch down to my face
to place an oval bud of lilac
briefly on my tongue
like the panda in central park
pink tongue testing
the succulence of the new growth
sensing its pent up energy
a green hum within
the tightly folded tissue of the plant
When spring comes I am
clean as a whistle
pissing pure Pellegrino
where are the chardonnays of yesterday
those golden goblets brimming with
the honeydew of France
and California long blonde
California thy pubic hair shaved
down to glittering bristle

legs slightly askew
and the fault line
glinting between them
we dive into the dark
as the buildings slide
into the sea.

Swell

Walking along Fifth Avenue
in the first warm light of this long winter
I feel the sun's rays talking to my blood
as I meander past each
ruined bank of phones
"Ride in a limo with naked blonde dancers"
says the sticker on every broken booth
and I juggle that busy scenario
in my head for several blocks
until I'm distracted by
heavy mendicant traffic around 53rd
I'm superstitious about beggars
I must elude three before I can pay one
and here they come in a bum's rush
beggar one sidestep and avoid eye contact
beggar two fake left and go right
number three according to his placard
is a blind diabetic
he only needs a quarter
but now his back is turned
as he hustles the shoppers descending
from Bergdorf's and Tiffany's
I walk past his outstretched mitt
with a clean conscience and a live quarter
that I have somehow earned
all I need is a working phone
maybe there is one by the Plaza
so I can contemplate
the perfect bronze haunches
of the statue of Abundance
while I'm talking to you
but you're not home
so I hang up the phone and go
examine the sweaters in Bergdorf's
like those other poets did
in Klein's one Christmas
years before I was in this city

65

and only dimly imagined
reeling up First Avenue/to fondle
soft sweaters/ and plump rumpled skirts
and now the author of those
lines has gone beyond
and his companion
on that lively walk
lies dying of the plague
It's in their honor that
I stroke the cashmere,
caress the lambswool
wallow discreetly
in the marvelous aromas
of the cosmetics department
a hundred perfumes
colliding in the air
as the genteel salesgirls cross
the floor their private lives
juicy as a cheerleader's diary
I genuflect briefly in praise
of older women in praise of
makeup both perfect and smeared
of all the subtle shades of red
that make their lips so luscious
they are characters from
a fiction of New York
inhabiting a parallel universe
that will never intersect with
the nine millimeter world
outside the door of this elegant store.

GUSH

When spring comes I'll piss in my hat
and have my alchemist turn it into coin
pay my bills and stun my creditors
rain and more rain, wash me clean
in the blood of the lamb
steer me clear of diss and discord
give me the upper body of
DeNiro in *Cape Fear*
I am turning into a big fat forty plus
a chewy cholesterolic
so serve me up some more
big dinners with hearty eaters
order the calve's liver forget the chicken
stick to the ribs
as the air around you thickens
with the glib remarks and flatulence
of diners in designer suits
clowns and frauds in suits
of lights with faulty wiring
they flicker like out of work christmas trees
third rate matadors feasting on the testicles
of bulls they did not earn
that never trampled tourists in Pamplona
disembowelled the picador's grey mare
devoured the benevolent cunya of Catalonia
or followed the curves of
Gaudi's handcarved staircase
to some Hispanic heaven
a darkened room at siesta
with murals by Goya
a white lace bedspread
and a map of young Spain stretched out
like a dancer on the feathery mattress…
More tapas waiter!
Another plate of balls here!
Churn up the consonants
get these words on the hoof.   67

It's Glenn O'Boogie's birthday
and he's furious that you have allowed
a mere blizzard to delay
your prompt arrival
the windows shake in their moorings
the bright flakes spinning
like rudderless vowels
in the sodium light
o's and a's and i's and you
helplessly twirling
waiting for the nail.

JIVE

Somewhere monks are
kneeling in prayer
as the dawn comes up
on their gleaming tonsures
a comforting smell of sheep and Jesus
radiating from woolly robes
but not on this street
there used to be trees on this block
nobody had their tongue in your purse
Diogenes sat in a barrel in
Washington Square
dispensing pills and wisdom
we sipped from a pool
of uncontaminated glee
wolfed endless supplies
of disco biscuits to keep
the horn rotating
if there was egg on my mug
it was only the residue of lunch
now every face in the crowd
moving down Broadway
seems so purposeful
going somewhere
with something to do
a whole generation
so much smarter than me
where was I when they were
handing out brains and ambition?
snorting toxins in the restroom
with the other ever readies
the assault & battery boys
burning down their house
and didn't even smell
the smoke of their credentials
going up in flames painting
the monkey with stolen lipstick
stabbing the crocodile

vacuuming up the last drops
of every dusty fragrance
reading the fine print on the porcelain
of a thousand toilet bowls
finally banished into "cold rosy dawn"
by spectral janitors
coughing and puking as they close
the creaking hinge of night.

I should demolish the tables
of the cardsharps and pickpockets
who ruin my daily stroll
along lower Broadway
with their felonious vibes
but the last time I stripped for action
at the gym everybody looked like
Hercules unchained so
I got dressed in a corner and
went home to ice cream and a video,
sorrowfully stroking the round white
curves of my imperfections.

Every day I mourn the lost body
but the heart races on
blood streaming through the ventricles
a solid boomdaboomdaboom
a beat you can dance to
loud enough to give my doctor
a small headache
as his silver stethoscope
checks my arterial pulse
smooth brown hand on my instep
tracking the cacaphony
of blood gunning through the body's tubes
"oh yes it's running well" he says
"a tendency to varicosity perhaps
but the artery is wide open"
a liquid avalanche careens through
subterranean passages

a tiny but perfectly formed
Raquel Welch surfing along
my femoral on a scarlet wave
I am dismissed with clean
health and a large bill
I walk out into the day
into a shiny moment
the light striking yellow cabs
and smoky redbrick walls
all movement specific and directed
infected by my optimism
order and civility briefly feasible
the garbage packed correctly
bottles cans and plastics stacked
the sidewalk suddenly clean
the dogs bark and their
owners pick up the tab
skaters surge past my left wing
in a fluid undulation of muscular grace
and I want my life like that
feet sliding lightly over the pavement
blood on the inside only,
the body's fragile urn intact and firm
moving through air.

THE PROCESSED LIFE

How do we maintain, sustain ourselves
in this world of knives and fire,
find a crack in the shroud
and squeeze through into that bright place
where words like "bejewelled"
are permitted, encouraged,
thimble, gombril, lantana
cyrillic, lanolin
sussuration, lapidary
they tumble from the tongue
and the poem is the sweet thing
quivering, a struck gong
and all I want is a sound like
immense oaken doors
slamming in sequence
down an endless marble hallway
and I want to believe what the poet said
what thou lovest well remains American
and this America stretching
away into blue distance
is a country of inventors and
adventurers artists and androids
crossdressers and clitlickers
wackos and maniacs of every stripe
but when I'm standing
on line in the supermarket
with my fellow Americans I feel
at one with Tonya Harding's people —
death rays from the planet
Jupiter have combined
with cheezits, franks and white bread
to transform us into
a homogeneous cluster
of gargantuan bodies
stuffed into our acid-washed jeans
slowly patrolling the over-stocked aisles
in search of the Caldor experience

the Walmart satori
prowling for bargains in patio furniture
among the sharp ozonic reek
of white noise and static
generated by acres of indestructible
chemical clothing
and irradiated fodder
protein-free meat from artificial animals
more plastic lawn chairs
than one nation could ever need.

Enormous televisions spray
a visible discharge of infotainment,
the braying of knaves and numbskulls
a sea of bland ectoplasmic faces
all merging into one toxic mugshot
as convincing and real as
the Pillsbury doughboy
Each gesture of harmony and
grace drowned out by
the tedious roar of commerce
and commercials interrupting
the live disaster shows
in which large white lawmen
bully small brown immigrants
caught with half a gram of coke
should they really be allowed
to break down your door
and shoot your dog for half a gram?
No, because this is America
everyone should have their own room,
and whatever's in that room
should be their own
we can no longer tell the difference
between what's sacred
and what's on sale
we're boxed up, bagelled
sea shook and shell shocked
hopping toward our exit   75

like a man in a sack with snakes
we will never recognise
old Mami Wata
when she slides onboard
speaking from bottles
and other containers
slipping her hook into our necks
with her silky verbs and peerless nouns
whispery linguistics
counting off our numbered days
brief lives fading like
smoke from an abbattoir.

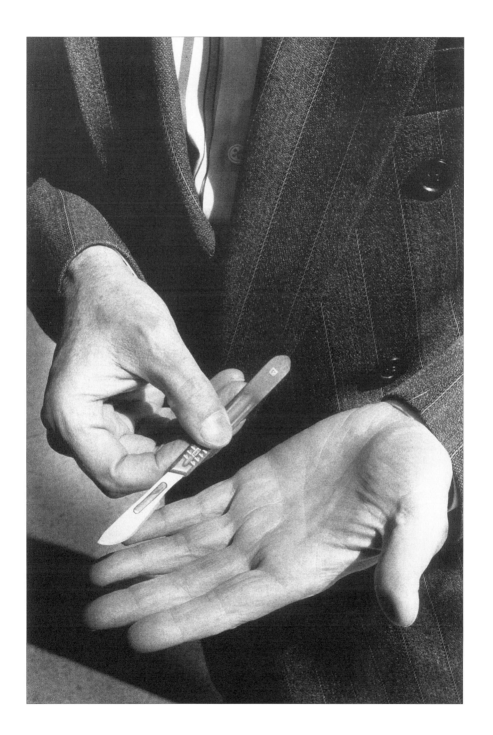

To What?

To what do I owe this insanitary napkin?
these rusted blades whirling through air?
I speak with the forked tongue
of a longchinned paleface
sauntering thru the lollapalaza
reeking of flowers and garlic
churlish music hums in my head
as the sun blinks out
and in again, banked behind
slate grey clouds
and gone again gone deep
as a spooked shark
as deep as my daughter's
pale blue eyes
"linger on / your pale blue eyes"
while I begin again
kneel down and start it up
my green heart
bold as a spring wired cardinal
strutting for foodchips
among the scuffed leaves
a hammered steel knight
of the three legs
rampant on a field
of mercury rising
lips loose and wrist stiff
as a busboy's arm fully
laden with dish and dishes
take me to your captain
let me lay it all on him
the gushy pulsing flow of it
the bloody red rag of it
the metal licking
gear grinding mess of it
open the throat

and spit out the emptiness
Ahab in the sky with lightning
a man without a meataxe
in a roomful of oxen.

BITTER TEARS

I got a letter from my liver
it said I want to live alone
all my organs have the power of speech
my ears always snarling "What's that??"
eyes unable to read the fine print
cock says "I'll stand up
when I feel like standing."
another appalling new sequence of
physical developments like the hair
growing out of my back
I was a smoothskinned monkeystunner
without a curve in the world
now I too am turning like the leaves
but words still pass like swords
through the esophagus
a blast furnace levels my nerves
shaping my intuitive grandeur into
something worth chewing on
small sections of the past
leap to the front of the head
wandering on the moors where
psychos buried tortured children
my mother held my hand
as if it would break
the wind a symphony of whispers
in which she heard the victims calling
their lamentations drifting
across the drystone walls
dividing the fields
into a green symmetry
I freed my hand from her pistol grip
when pubic hair arrived went
looking for love in market towns
trawling for scrubbers with
Watson and Quambro
fuelled up nightly at the
Crown or the Vine

and departed on all fours
inebriated lion cubs
trespassing into the foreign precincts
of Sheffield and Lincoln
the dangers of Doncaster
Quambro's rickety Ford Prefect
side swiping country bumpkins
in clapped out Zephyrs
or was it an Anglia that
pursued us in barley–fuelled rage
along pitch–black roads
finally cornered in a farmyard
A quid for the paint
Quambro kept repeating
between smirks to the furious driver
his passenger had already
removed his shirt
torso glistening in the Ford's headlights
as he assumed a combat stance but
Watson broke his jaw with a right hook
as he was climbing from the car
First punch counts, cunt!
he danced away to a neutral corner
then leaped across
to strike the startled driver
laid *him* out flat in the chickenshit
a sudden violent reversal
pressed their faces into
muck and gravel and blood
He's up! he's down! squawked Quambro
in manic ringside commentary
our laughter tearing holes in the dark
Watson flexed his couch-toting arms
bare knuckle warrior
bathed in the ghostly radiance
of the lights teeth glittering
sharp as a fox's mouth fresh from
the massacre of domestic fowl
a dim frieze of antic figures

in a winter landscape
bodies humming with animal
contempt for damage and loss
we left the punched-out chumps
and drove into the dawn
ravenous for fish and chips
and cheese and chutney sandwiches.

Double Bill

Prowling the market square
after our weekly dose of celluloid
pumped up by pillage and
ruin with The Vikings
mimicking the arrogance
of Kirk Douglas or the
dimpled sneer of Tony Curtis
(an unlikely heir to the
throne of Northumbria)
beat pirates striding the decks
as the ocean moves beneath them
going someplace that this town will
never take us its tiny dimensions
shrinking with each small cultural infusion
Kirk has a perfectly developed
torso and an attitude to match
his proclivity for violence and travel
an inspiration to landlocked
small-town youth and when
Tony's falcon takes out Kirk's eye
he simply chokes the bird
and slaps a patch
over the bloody vacancy
as the longships sail on
to trembling coastal kingdoms
foreign ports teeming with something
closer to our idea of "life" where
all the men are cowards and
all the women look like
Rita Hayworth in *Gilda*
tossing her hair back on the balcony
of a lavish hacienda
the essence of juice induction
the electric charge of her screen presence
creates a surge of pure desire
that passes like a wave
through the darkened cinema

you can sense the suppression of raw need
as a muzzled intake of breath
in the next seat
stirring the blood pudding
of half-formed bodies
circuit overload jolting the
adolescent epicenter
pineal gland bulging in its socket
thighs crossed tight to contain
the sheer thrust of muscle and boner
she shakes her hair down
it falls caressingly
across her face and the laser
gaze of her dark eyes
guides rockets with your name
stencilled across
their gleaming steel surfaces
directly into the cavernous
aperture gaping in your chest where
your heart has already exploded.

JACK THE LAD

Yesterday the hot water heater blew up
and now the house is filled with surly plumbers
unaware that my father was a plumber
a man who knew how to melt down lead
but never figured out how to turn it into gold
Was it his absence of alchemy
that made these empty pockets my inheritance?
How stylish to blame my late father
for my financial situation he's dead
and long gone he took me to the circus once
Chipperfield's pitched its tent in Chesterfield
a sixty mile roundtrip by bus
and that was all the time he could spare
from his busy social calendar
each night he stood in front
of the kitchen mirror
to tie his bow tie with
a self-taught elegance
slow gestures of authentic grace
dressed in soft viyella and
tweed and cavalry twill
the full regalia of a gentleman
for that ten minute walk
to the Flying Scotsman
though he didn't drink that much
and only got nasty on Sunday lunchtime
because of the proximity of Monday
when he would be back
on that bicycle loaded
with his sack of tools
frost on his knuckles
coattails flying in the dawn
headed for another impossible tangle
of base metals on the underside
of somebody's filthy sink
he slipped a fiver into my hand
when I left home for London

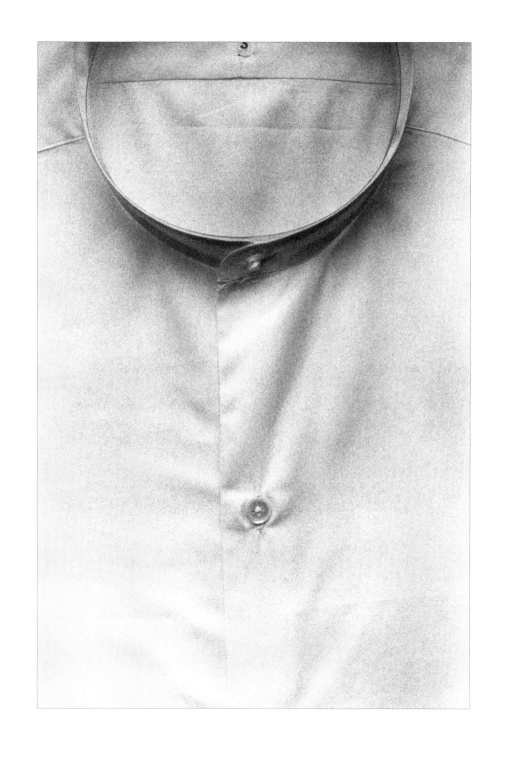

it wasn't much but it meant a lot
it paid for the cigarettes
I smoked while travelling
toward that delinquent Parnassus
where I was convinced
dirty blondes would
tamper with the brakes
of my chariot and insist
that I stay just a little bit longer
in their sweet smelling stables
let me sleep all night in their soul kitchens
but I soon discovered most bedsitters
didn't even have kitchens
and all the blondes had
homely-looking roommates who
never left the house.

July (Heat)

In dreams I fondle blonde
reporters from the *Times*
their breasts are globular
and smeared with newsprint
those shapes sustain me through
these battery-operated days
the pavement unyielding
as fragile glass decanters
slide from my hands and
shatter on the sidewalk
the explosion punching me
back into the world
like a fish snatched
from cool green depths
into an airless christian morning
to discover that
Lana Turner has once again collapsed
and she won't soon be getting up
thirty years after Frank's request
to "get up, Lana, we love you!"
she has taken her last breath
gone to join Johnny and Lex and
Artie Shaw and all the other exes
I read her obituary in the green silence
of the park after a summer shower
the air exhaling a temporary purity
as I move along toward my own last sigh
mouth uttering feeble instructions
to arrest or somehow delay
this rapid forward motion
extend the luxury of finding air
and breathing space
before the brief years elapse
and a paragraph in the newspaper
is all that constitutes a spent life.

The Fourth

The rank odor of July begins to build
on the 4th day cordite mingles
with stale sweat, oily puddles
of unspeakable liquid
ornament the pavements
a slimy reptilian gloss
on the sidewalk
hcat flares like the fireworks
exploding over the Battery
a crowd hurried pell-mell
toward the water
faces caught in the rainbow
glare of ordnance
my daughter freaked by
crazy patterns in the sky
the fugitive glances and guttural
staccato of a gathering mob
the madness of crowds
looming on a summer night
she pointed directly toward Home
M80s burst loud as gunshots
a security crew rushed past us
into the projects that cluster
in this southeastern sector
the neighbourhood totally unfamiliar
the artificial yellow light
resembled a crime scene
waiting for perpetrators
we were right beneath a bridge
I couldn't tell which bridge
a cab drifted by like a lifeboat
we jumped aboard
and sailed back through
the dull explosions
to our part of the breathing world.

The Sixth

I went downstairs into the sixth day
determined to make this month
undulate and shake its bluntshaped booty
inhale the filthy armpit of a city summer
accept the polyester texture of the heat
but rational thought blisters
into little pockets of goof
sense of the mind skidding on concrete
on this section of the journey
the road hits you back
my friend's life unravels
inside another heatwave
a provincial summer
in the English Midlands
goldfish dying in the pond
the lawn scorched past saving he
calls me long distance with the details
of his distress and I can't help him
there's nothing new in his sad story
thousands imploding every day
when the mail arrives and
love has turned into a letter bomb.

The Tenth

The thermometer yawns into three figures
cattle are on their udders in the midwest
in Chicago the bodies overflowed the morgue
refrigerated trucks stood humming at the curb
loading up the heat-struck victims
Bring out your dead sang the EMS technicians
and I am astonished to find myself still alive
at the other end of the electronic tube
amazed at the casual proximity of disaster
a teabag discovered like a body at the
bottom of my cup
the sadness of these tiny leather sandals
waiting to be occupied and re-animated
by a singular presence
solid heat pours down
the chimney of the skull
and nothing works right
the powerbook blinks out
the phone is mute
the camera flips its shutter
doors refuse to close without
the assistance of an angry boot.

The trick to this month
is simply staying alive
weaving through the sodden murk
like a dancer in a minefield
stranded at the doctor's
or in the waiting room
of the car repair shop
reading about all the beautiful
people in *Vanity Fair*
while the technician checks
the result of my cat scan
or the barium enema
he administered to my crankcase
pray that the gasket is sealed

the brain devoid
of malignancy and tumour.
I am clean this time
but someone did get their share
of bad news as the sun bore down
and life changed immensely
in a moment
in the space between sentences
and I can only repeat the mantric
line from Eluard
singing the great joy and how
beautiful you look in my white shirts
single needle longstaple
handsewn Egyptian cotton
caressing the bare skin like that cool
sheet covering your nakedness
on this humid afternoon
this is what is mine
this is what drives life along this is
what I want to say I would
lay down my life for
the force that illuminates me
from the inside out
that which subjects me
to such agony and glee
thee and thee.

The Fifteenth

On Hudson street
my eye was wandering as
my head rotated like a camera
searching out perfection
in a defective landscape
suddenly focussed on
the delicate limbs of
an oriental woman
standing in line
at the Korean grocery
bright red toenails on elegant feet
strapped into high heel sandals
I bought milk and juice and
soon picked up the trail
of her pedals perambulating
slowly down North Moore
they were so alluring
pristine above the melting tarmac
I almost made a remark
like "nice feet" or "cool nail polish"
but realized in time
it might sound
as weird as it was beginning to feel
sloping down the street
in my tightfitting t-shirt
I fit the description of a creep.

The Twenty-third

An American family conforming
exactly to the stereotype
climbs from a Chrysler
with out-of-state plates
looking for a reasonably priced
hamburger in Soho on a Saturday night
father's got polyblend shorts
thick legs and blue socks
like those stroke models in
the new scratch'n' sniff Calvin Klein ads
his boy's face an explosion of acne
from daily handgunning practice
inspired by those same ads
and daughter's wearing a
Hole t-shirt and a sweet smile
has dad heard *Live Through This*
faintly thru the wall
of the ranch house as
the heat cloisters the suburbs
into a throbbing hive
of sexual turmoil
ready to erupt like
the boil on his son's
tightly wound neck?

News From Abroad

In a stand of fragrant trees she
looped her belt around a branch
and swung out into space
a girl barely begun and already gone
I am swimming in a pool in sunlight
my voice still safe in my throat
and the refugees have watched their sons
and husbands led away to slaughter
"killed the boys and the luggage
'tis expressly against the rules of war"
sympathy seems banal but it is all I have
I can't spend too long imagining
my larynx sawn away by butchers' knives
I am safe in a green garden in blue July
as the light descends exquisitely to evening
and there is nothing deadly in the dark
no-one approaching down the road
carrying my murder in their grimy hands.

The beach shone beneath the stars
three clouds hung over the ocean
like gigantic faulty lampshades
filled with lightning
electricity flaring inside
their gossamer volumes
we lay back and watched
this celestial show
with our friends and our children
and our fine food and wine
in between courses
I tried to say a prayer for
the refugees moving over mountains
the people of Zepa of Szrebenica
impossible names on an impossible map
the Balkan dance of death
so far from this rapturous Atlantic night
there is no music in Bosnia

there is no mercy in
the news of the world
that quality abandoned
in those ancient mountains
all hope devoured
by maniacs rancid with slivovitz
the clouds over this island
contained the body electric
madness was elsewhere
and the night lapped around us
briefly inhabiting a cooler region
of water and sand
as the heat out there
smothered movement
and common sense
this is all that happened,
the weather the ocean
the news from abroad.

STROLL

1.

On Canal street the golden fields
in the Marlboro billboard
catch the slanting autumn light
in perfect mimesis of
a carcinogen free reality
this intersection is always
a perilous crossing a seething
convergence of rubber and steel
one false step can put you
in harm's way your
destiny written in lipstick
on the exhaust pipe
of a fish truck from Delaware
frail flesh merging
with a Volvo's chrome
another sacrifice to
the lord of the crossroads
whose name is constantly
erased and rewritten
in the glutinous shifting tarmac
by an endless stream of vehicles
carrying food and lumber
and frozen goods to Brooklyn
and the lands beyond.

2.

The grinding yellow cabs
roar up Sixth in tight formation
"so many pedestrians so little time"
inscribed in Urdu on their dashboards
rage held precariously in check by Nusrat
Khan's voice like Himalayan streams
cooling the riot boiling in their necks
oh mighty city most glamorous town
I kiss thy star flecked feet
between the filthy toes

where the meat smell lingers
after the tables have been
taken in from the terrace
and the cats fight over
the leftover pompano
outside *da Silvano.*

3.
Crossing Seventh to St Luke's
Place where we conducted our
first holy moaning matrimonials
experiments in peonies and lace
I put my lips to the brick
faking a private anguish as a lady
steers her snarling dog around
my kneeling form.

4.
The familiar contours of Hudson Street
lead me by irresistible pork pies
glistening in Myers' window
the lard-rich pastry evokes a Proustian flash
an entire civilization that no longer exists
the English working class.

5.
Taza de Oro the cup of gold
where the rat fell out of the ceiling
into Rachid's soup the same week
he had the dead dog delivered
to his restaurant in the rush hour
and the Irish Yakuza
trashed his new saloon
our lives were measured then in
random acts of sex and violence
on that night the fresh snow
covering 8th Avenue
invoked a brief pastoral silence
while behind the etched glass doors

the antique mahogany
counter of the bar
splintered with a scream
as molecules dispersed
beneath the axeblows of hooligans.

        6.
The streets down here are lined with
fresh fools each old garage
transformed into a bistro
a cash machine within screaming distance
of every karmic sinkhole a Banana Republic
to clothe the bland leading the bland
meekly into the millenium
the town seems overloaded with movies
I haven't seen and bars I haven't drunk in
I got drunk in other places home and away
so many facedown moments last summer
steam rising like smoke from wet grass
as another barely digested dinner
was violently returned to earth
in the background the polite
murmur of the other guests
ignoring my convulsions
all the church basements were
calling out to me to come
and declare my dependence
and Bacchus with his foot on my head
let me up o Lord of the bottle
and I shall drink water for a month
but Bacchus is annoyed at my arrogance
his deerskin slipper flips me over
on my back helpless as a crab
ghost fingers down my throat
explore the far reaches of the
pancreas churning up the fungal
mix he squeezes the bile duct
and a fresh gush of dark juices
drench the foliage

the septic stew pours out
in a roaring belch
that my hostess will recall for years
in polite conversation
pointing out the darker circles
on her immaculate lawn
where the acid of my innards
scorched the bluegrass
and charred the mole-free fescue.

7.
Across the river
an absence of bliss
in the garden state
tankers roll off the turnpike
like demented beasts of burden
cracking under the strain of the mineral
waste strapped to their backs, exploding
in the middle of this shining
afternoon adding fire to the leaves
already burning out in sugar overload
the guttering light of early November
when Cookie's flame merged with the sun
seven years have passed since she
vanished into light rising like mercury
into a silvery vacancy
the memory of her face still sharp
as toothache an absolute
blonde who would never turn brown
no matter how long
she lay in the sun
of Provincetown and Positano
throat loaded with
laughter over some dopey joke
in our last chance encounter
on Bleecker street before
she was swallowed up by hospitals
to begin the technical process of dying.
Some people sink instantly

from consciousness
dead or alive and others take up
permanent residence in the memory bar
mixing forbidden cocktails
with the same complete abandon
that characterised their lives
and why you loved them
everything and anything is permitted
now that the tedious physical journey
has ended and a longer voyage begun
they sip their beakers of lightning
and reminisce about their
brief transit through this incarnation
musing without regret
on what might have been
what and who they did and didn't do
vaguely perplexed to
suddenly find themselves
pausing in the gleaming interior
of a divine sepulcher and
hardly went to church
in their lives unsure of the protocol
in this vast cathedral that also contains
a four-star restaurant and
the latest facilities for
time and space travel
everyone is *here to go.*

    8.
Waiting for the new moon to surface
behind the fake Tuscan belltower
of our Lady of the weeping Virgins
we gambled in their basement
high on mescaline the dollar bills
like petrified cardboard
as they slid across the cheap baize
of the tables run by mannish nuns
your pearls looked real and the cops
looked suspicious when

you grabbed some guy's tie
and demanded "Is that real?"
the night was full of grabby hands
on Bleecker Street the fortune
teller snatched your cash
and it simply disappeared into the
rubbery folds of her bosom
irretrievable was the word that popped out
like a sign you had stars
on your forehead and your eyes
were glowing blue as neon
as you wrestled the money back
extracted it with those
long surgical fingers
from the gypsy's mammary grip
and left her marking another Tarot deck
we don't need predictions about the future
while we teeter in chemical space
with holes in our flightsuits
circling Chinatown for hours
searching for the perfect
chop suey landing zone.

9.
A million beautiful breathing moments
like this one approaching again
purple light draping the tenement walls
pigeons strut and tourists roost on benches
enchanted by the rhythm that moves
this cast of characters through the streets
the soft billowy eloquence of a woman
traversing the avenue
a dozen worshippers tuned to
her pherenomic signals
the pavement is a house of prayer
for one brief instant before the thunder
of uptown traffic swirls by like cavalry
bare arms long legs the smell of coffee
and paprika the rich grease of giros

congealing in the windows
of Mohammedan food parlors
cumulus blushing pink in
the last light from Jersey
a jetliner rides safely into the darkness
the proximity of the church
fills me with a vicarish instinct
wishing safe journey home
for all who must travel
in planes or trains on land at sea
for everyone a peaceful trip
even these cowboys from Queens
in an ancient Camaro
running a red light at Waverley Place.

     10.
A schooner of Blanche de Brooklyn
cream of wheat beer
appears at my elbow
and the evening disappears
in amber waves that wash
the shirt from your shoulders
the shadows in the
cusp of your neck
fit themselves around
the snout of my long glance
your opalescent eyes
a dream of the
clean sheets of home.

MIDTOWN

Poncey English actors upstage each other
in the vestibule of another
cramped audition space
conducted by a sad old drama major
always the understudy never the bride
reduced like us to small horizons
spewing uninflected nonsense
into a microphone with
only minor resonance
pitching for soaps and
cars and telephones
I recognise one hackneyed face
among these folding chairs
doing schtick with the competition
the Indian accent
now the tired Italian reruns
the receptionist puts on her headphones
didn't he live with some old tart
like Joan Collins a few years back
they did a play together
short run poor reviews
all our stars are faded
in this holding tank
we get up sheeplike
when our names are called
enter the sound-proof box
to perform our verbal softshoe
trying to get hard for sinks and soap
and valves and vaseline
the systole and diastole
the lumbar puncture repair kit
the exfoliating fluid
with built in hair care
that everyman must
apply to his shanks
to improve his standing his

station eclipse the neighbours'
pretensions with the larger
dimensions of his own personal style
bad copy bounces off the walls
the shrill and petulant one-liners
of artists trapped in admens' bodies
the voice trapped like Cocteau's
human voice in a box of static
squawks and fades into
the soundproof walls
my timeless interpretation
dissected by a panel of yesmen
rejected by corporate salamanders
who underestimate my capabilities
but it's still early in the day
the casting director dismisses me
with a vestige of the sneer he once had
before sinking into this morass
of mindless commerce and easy cash.

Outside the sun shines on the billboards for
Barrymore and a dozen other plays
currently electrifying
the women of Scarsdale
gaffers and hoofers scurrying
through the stage door
with cheap coffees
while the male lead sips a latte
and oils his vocal cords
with the sweat of pageboys
procured by defrocked curates
in strange rituals of the theater
alluded to but never quite revealed
in the memoirs of the great queens
who pranced upon these boards
their baroque genius
igniting my resentful adoration
their flagrant insincerity
pulling the queer triggers
that attract me mothlike
to their swishy brilliance.

On Ninth Avenue the food stores
perfume the sidewalks with
saltcod stockfish herbs and spices
beyond my culinary grasp
the taxis braying South
don't touch their brakes
hack radar sensing my lack of readies
eight dollars in my pocket
and another cheap lunch in sight
the E train carries me down to
Said's Egyptian chicken overload
it's a wide world and
I'm spreading into it.

'70s (Slight Return)

My daughter offered me a hundred
dollars to eat a dead moth
she must have learned that from
her mother always insisting
I eat live things on a dare
caterpillars and flies served up
on leaves but I just couldn't
crunch that spidermeat
like I would have in
the bent frame of youth
when I understood nothing
and drank everything
while I was waiting in the wings
for something to begin
to kick in to be real gone again
waiting on the starving actors
who cluttered the booths at
Phebe's on the Bowery all of them
destined for misfortune
unless they got a real job they
dream on subways now of
that last curtain call
applause rich as velvet fading into
the latticework of morning
as the train pulls into
the underworld of
Grand Central Station
there was no art in life just
raw bodies colliding in
the chemical night
soft explosions of lust and
battery eclipsing the civilized as
the years poured down the drain
echoes of that loveless tune
still resound through the
hallways of the Hotel Chelsea
epidural center of a numb youth

the hum of true bohemia
coursing through the building
pulled me right off the banks
and ducked me in the river
of underground USA
washed me down in the blood of a wig
I knew what I would find there
as I swam through the corridors
beguiled by pale submariners
who plied their cunty trade
with a feral resolution
their trapdoors opened
like the jaws of life
I tumbled down their mohair stairs
to land on piles of drugs and threadbare
floors of factories retooled for heels and
whores with golden holes for
hearts and daughters who
would later work at Scores
they were bigger than *Life* magazine
veterans of a thousand mimeo parties
undressing in rooms with a view
and basements in the dark
re-enacting for the squares
nocturnal clashes in the park with
minotaurs who prowled the
spikestrewn lawns and lay
in wait beyond the railings
to relieve the harried citizens
of whatever cash and
chattels they could resell for dope
a dollar for your life in hallways
enamelled with the texture
of a nightmare and when this
innocent new arrival asks what
New York was really like back then
I reply without exaggeration
"Utter heaven."

Paris, France

For the second time in a day
I lied about my age
I could feel Anita's eyebrows
moving skyward behind me
as I glibly deducted a couple of years
grinning through yellow horse teeth
a Jean Seberg festival was
playing at the Forum
what kind of car was she parked in
when they found her
must have been a Peugeot
or maybe that Citroën that
looks like a crouching frog
I loved her in *Breathless*
selling the *Herald Trib*
to a big-lipped Belmondo
and Paris looked so great in
black and white I love Paris
but the French are hard to love
with these exceptions:
Hotel La Louisiane room number 9
a vision seen through a cloud of steam
a young Charlie Parker lookalike
nailing Anita Pallenberg
when she was a simple odalisk
a Scandinavian fertility symbol
this place is drenched in past
and future sex and we follow
these phantoms suits on the floor
near the door our bodies colliding in
a flurry of foie gras energy
below the photograph of Cendrars
in front of his tiny typewriter
one armed bandit smashing the keys
into exquisite lines signed in
that corrosive left handed scrawl
when we went to honor his memory   117

in a grey suburban cemetery
beneath the freeway at Batignolles
his ashes had been removed
where are the cinders of Cendrars?
I asked the gardien a mad Clouseau
dripping with red wine hangover
the sister has taken the casket
I think he said
he offered to show us Breton's grave
instead but we don't care much
for André too bossy and he was rude
to Frida Kahlo who also said
he smelled very bad
both attributes so very French
especially that whiplash tongue
we're so American in our ablutions
the story of eau in our circular room
we like our scented baths almost as much as
the Pomerol perfumed with
hayfields and autumn valleys
voluptuous as the dense black skirts
of Corot's peasants at the Musée d'Orsay
walking back in the rain
along the Rue de Seine
I conjure the artists out of the air
Léger and Braque and
Picasso round the corner on Grands-Augustins
The Delaunays Sonia and Robert
painting the same Paris that's in
my periscope this morning
slate roofs shiny as the grey silk lining
of Alain Delon's Borsalino
raised in salute to Bob le Flambeur
at the Gare du Nord and Alfred
Jarry smiles at Eluard and
Théophile Gautier and Jean-Paul Gaultier
Gérard Depardieu and Cardinal Richelieu
and the *Quatre Cents Coups*
of François Truffaut

Rififi and Fifi the poodle and Coco Chanel
Jean Genet and Bertrand Blier
Notre Dame and votre femme
in the afternoon while
you're fixing the Citroën
thinking about the cancan
misunderstanding Jacques Lacan
and Molière's school for scandal
and Molyneux and Molly Bloom
chez Sylvia Beach a kiss
to Sylvia for delivering *Ulysses*
an explosion of genius
barely contained by its sky-blue covers
and I bow to Apollinaire
head wrapped in bandages like a dying king
at the beginning of the 20th century
and Doisneau in the banlieue
and Balzac and de Sade in the same breath
as Sylvie Vartan and Sylvie Haymann
spending quiet days in Clichy
and Sylvie Sabatier shiny as a blade
and Simone Signoret making a cassoulet
and Jeanne Moreau serves a soufflé
All the gorgeous Parisians cooking
and making love through
the long winter nights reading Baudelaire
and Brigitte Bardot's memoirs
watching double bills
of Godard and Melville
and Paris is a city that
remembers its dead
JP Roland-Levy is dead
by miscalculation and Coluche
is dead by motorcycle
and Guillaume Gallozzi
true Bohemian
from an insult to the brain
and the philosopher
struck down by an ambulance

in the midst of a perfect pensée
and Queneau and Perec
and Madame Gres
but Cartier-Bresson lives on
and Anouk Aimée wearing Cartier
shimmers on the Champs-Elysées
and I'll never read Foucault
much less Baudrillard
give me my Rimbaud and
the glory of the Tower
a glittering epiphany of orange light
seen from a drunken boat cruising
the dark waters of the Seine
its corpses weighed down by
Céline's manuscripts
they even left the lights on
in the Louvre and if I wasn't
right here in this church
I'd like to be climbing
the slopes of Montparnasse
with a bottle and a glass
or eyeballing the tumescent flanks
of the marble horses in the
Luxembourg gardens
and the discreet beauty of the nannies
secrets wrapped around them like
the cashmere that covers
the children in their care.

We sip the golden beer of March
inside this waterside bar
as the winter sun flames out
Notre Dame framed
in ancient magnificence
behind your Schiapparelli head.

DANCE FARM

to Jane

Blink and the ache is gone
full possession of the senses is a fine thing
but wine is a fine thing too
it's a part of life like the ocean is
almost identical in composition to
human blood I read somewhere
at night the planets dance I read that too
but what ancient books fed me
these instructions
what provides my sound
when I feel my instrument
waking up at this table
lungs full of air
air full of light
I put the mouthpiece to my lips
and try to bring some gravy home
I want to leave my mark
pin some small emblem
to the velvet cloak
a shard a glimmer a sonic spark
put some nectar in your glass
a jewel and some juice
before my tail lights disappear
into the dark and the night
falls open like a knife
eternity blue air rushes by
all the clichés are polished and they
respond to the insistent pumping
of my furious elbow
my muzzle has been removed
I take a man size bite of terra firma
spitting earth into gymnastic acrostics
instructions for the dance
the spirit of the clavicle triggers
signals to those well fed stars

gravity has cut me loose
I will loop my body into a Mobius strip
elasticate my fugue stance
churn my spine into snakes
a supple liquidity
replacing the Reichian ridgepole
that holds my shoulders up
unlock and load and glide down
the curve of the world
in rammerjammer hipshake
simpatico unison
with the rhythm of big mother earth.

I want to dance in Jane's comfort
I want a grant to create my own dance farm
where nubile students
will mow the vast lawns in textbook
arabesques of social realism
I'll direct from the seat of my John Deere
cruel and brilliant as Balanchine
my arms ropy with muscle
calves like bludgeons
superbly indifferent
to the lepidopteral attentions
of the swarming ballerinas.

SNAPSHOTS

1. *Shopping Crimes*

I fucked the salesgirl in the back
among the discount winter coats
it was fast and dismal for both of us
decided not to take the jacket after all
outside the store a plump blonde
Transit cop eased herself
from a patrol car with
an odd feline grace
and I felt the urge to confess
to be cuffed and cross-examined
to spill my beans into
the voluminous breasts
concealed beneath her
polyester battle dress.

2. *Beach Scene*

She called the baby Lino
after Lino Ventura nobody
in America knows who he is
Lino's mother was complaining
she had nipples like doorbells
and Lino was busily ringing
them as she talked.

3. *The Mystery of Fashion*

In a riverrine dream
we glided down
the liquid corridor of the Amazon
she had traded her Balenciaga
for magic herbs
the witch doctor looked divine
in that Parisian drag
it had arrived where it belonged
we understood the
true meaning of a cocktail dress

4. *Nerve Bindings*

Another day moved
through its brief stations
geese were crossing a snowy sky
a crow chanted like a monk
on the perimeter of the field
I smashed an egg into the pan
and flipped it in a gumbo arc
trapped it slapped it and
fed it to the child
roaring through the stop signs
of my morning
the enormous comfort of bright yolk
oozing into fresh Italian bread
temporarily dispersing the armies
of anxiety and distress
massing ant-like under my hump.

5. *Dear Abby*

Don't presume I'm homosexual
just because I run my fingers
across your shoulders
or caress your triceps
with an errant hand on this
voluptuous summer evening
I'm merely jealous of your
body's building and
the odious comparison
my ruined temple makes
my precipitous decline
from a monkey to a sloth
a nicely toned arm inside
a merino sleeve the gauge of
the muscle and the wool
are two of life's more sensual pleasures
so I'm not afraid to stroke them
even if we're not near
as queer as we seem.

6. *Story Hour*

Open the throat it's the speaking season
not the hunting season water
tumbling on a rock is
Casanova's gushy dam everything
performed in honor of something my
rope dance climbs into the sky while
you drink up Molly Bloom
the woman's point of view miraculously
evoked by a panty-sniffing man.

7. *The Great Escape*

Brainstorms from hashfires lit up the
grey North London landscape
the voice of Lenny Bruce
pierced the creeping damp
a tidal wave of sonic delight
denting the karma of those
cramped rooms opening the third eye
wide enough to see there was
no alternative to immigration.

8. *Country Comforts*

A set of gardening tools incites
the horn to rise in simple Japanese
pants available by mail from
the pseudo-English supply company
the curve of a scythe the teeth of a saw
what hammers here bolt upright
in the straw among the rusting bikes
and dysfunctional lawn tractors
echoes of other summers call the onanist
to order amid the chaos of aging steel
sperm jets across a rake's smooth handle
dust motes swirl in lazy arcs
through bands of light
as the sun moves on from
station to station.

9. *Acid*

In Norfolk England on a
lysergic autumn night
the voice of Marilyn Monroe
came drifting through the ether
followed by a Polish newscast
announcing her birthday
or the anniversary of her demise
I couldn't decipher the harsh
Slavic syllables
but it was good to know
she was remembered
so fondly in the Eastern bloc.

10. *Manners*

Shaving at the sink I resemble
my father at last
the best dressed plumber
in Nottinghamshire
who occasionally farted
with great nonchalance
while attending to his toilette
my mother's darting glance
of pure disgust
enough to teach me
bathroom etiquette for years.

11. *Bogus*

Looking at the painter
framed in the doorway of the gallery
I knew all he had really done
was to figure out the money part
like I looked at the coyote in Pasadena
and knew I could do what he did
though I don't have the jaws yet
wolf thoughts drifting and
nothing but sheep out on the foam
drizzle the oil over the roast
says the unctuous chef
with a fatty smirk
It is a facile world when chefs
rule empires are featured
on the front pages of national
newspapers when they take over
entire neighbourhoods
and charge enormous sums
for fragments of their
genius expressed in bread
and three dollar muffins
it's all in the eyes and the PR and
when I looked in the painter's eyes
I saw the word "bogus"
in italics behind the name
"Armani" on the frame.

12. *Mexico*

Tequila herradura the horseshoe
in the back of the head a palomino
trampling the frontal lobes
Mexico was scary after dark
but I was too drunk
to be totally terrified
the local people addressed my
brother Juan as "Don Juan"
he was an artist and this
probably kept us from being lynched
or robbed there were no police
and no streetlights in Tepotzlan
Juan was trying to crossbreed a chicken
with a hawk to create
an invincible fighting cock
but every time they put the chicken
in the cage the hawk killed it
each bird sat with its death a few minutes
while the breeders hoped for a miracle
of consummation but the hawk would
rather fight than fuck and
furious at his incarceration struck
each chicken down with one quick stroke
Juan smiles a Tijuana smile
and hands the body to the cook.

13. *Fugue State*

My fugue state a flugelhorn
unclogged at last like the tubes that thread
their delicate routes around my insides
worn down from years of overload
revived by herbs and medications
advertised in the *Post* alongside
breathless accounts of sodomite cops
people are shocked as if this
had never happened before
it's only our white skin that curbs
their psychotic insolence raw meat
closer to the bone than
you ever want to know
if you're not cut you won't bleed
the spell I weave each day
around my loved ones
not cut won't bleed
not touched by any harm
throw the ring of power
round the aura radiating
from my daughter's body
reassuring as a stove's clean heat
or the solid rhythm of Arsene's heart
as he stepped from the
waves and placed my
hand to his watercooled chest
to feel the divine machinery
driving the blood through
his small clean veins so utterly alive
inside that pulsating moment
of victory over the sea.

14. *X-Files*

The negative vivacity of my neighbour's
ghastly imagination doubles back to give him
the horrors when he gets a shot
of post–operative painkiller—they've extracted
a hernia the size of a grapefruit or
bound it up in nylon netting
so it won't explode and choke him with blood—
I tuned out the detailed description
delivered by his unsympathetic wife
who remains unmoved by his visions of flames
pouring from electrical outlets
basketball players transforming into rodents
on his glowing TV screen extraterrestrials
scurrying into corners of the room
all the terrors of acid with nothing of the joy
imagination expanding into ruin
the god of panic has taken the reins
and given the old catholic
a generous foretaste of the afterlife.

15. *The Night*

Put another camper on the fire
to keep the mountain lions
at bay to warm the hooves of the
horses standing in the imaginary mist
of a fictional western night
abandon the garbage and the lawn
to their pale suburban devices
sit by that fire and stare into the flames
see America falling into place
choice cuts and prime rib roasting
adding more layers to the fat
a cat leaps at the window like
a panther in the rain
the glass holds him like it holds
back the night a slim wafer
of protection against the wild world
swarming in the gunsight
the bowel-melting click of
a shotgun slide in an empty house
what every thief should hear
upside their felonious head
"Hold it right there" spoken
without a quaver as convincingly as
Sam Shepard standing on the corner of
Houston Street tall as Gary Cooper
all American perfectly capable of saying
"fill your hand" to any gun-toting criminal
how do you keep the weight off Sam
keep that lean machine ticking and
tricking the gods into thinking
you have a long time coming
before you go?

16. *In Search of the Miraculous*

We are not asking for miracles simply
demanding the signs that indicate the
possibilities of altered states the intrusion
of the absurd into the everyday each
time the birds fly to the right of my
eyescreen I breathe in I exhale more
clearly convinced that something good
will happen even if
the phone rings and there is
nobody on the line.

17. *Bitter Recall*

You were the skater on the lawn
bundled against the February chill
or was it already March
when you posed for me
in front of the old maple
a photograph that would surface
years later as evidence of something
more than a desert
where only snakes lived,
and solitaries sneering
at golden opportunities.

18. *Doreens*

A clean blue day presents itself
in my southern hemisphere
and Ecuadoreans
we call them Doreens
who were once supple boys diving
from clifftops for tourists
put new glass in my windows
providing a clear view of the blue
and the white gulls turning into gold
as they catch the sun's last rays
an optical miracle squeezed into my
sightbox aerodynamically perfect
shapes transfigured by the light
suspended in the absolute
clarity of air.

19. *Perfect Curve*

The fingernail left on my desk
invokes the slim astonished shape
of the hand it once adorned
distant fingers lithe as the eels
gasping in my cooler for tonight's
striped bass maneuvers.

20. *Close Encounter*

On a darkened country road
two girls riding a bicycle
stolen from the artist who
had recently failed to seduce them
with his paint-stained evocations
of Bohemia were halted by
the sudden appearance of
a spaceship which blocked their path
and froze them in their tracks
they lay there terrified
while an extraterrestrial snurge
composed entirely of nostrils and light
voluptuously examined the saddle.

21. *Enlightenment*

Meat is murder but
I eat it screaming
like a bacon painting into
the frozen void
of sunday afternoon
all normal here
gardens frantic with produce
orchards loaded with gleaming fruit
the green lawn not sinister
crows flying to the left not
sinister I'm not receiving
messages through my fillings
the mercury deposits
gathered from my previous
incarnation as a hatter
saintly, mad, obese
on Ludlow street
a hundred years ago.

22. *The Girl from Ipanema*

The fire cracks like
gunshots in the stove
hard maple from that tree
torn in two by forked lightning
the night Silvia danced
beneath the storm-whipped branches
fearless "nymph of fields
and standing woods"
arms raised into the deluge
mouth open in glorious laughter
she defied the lightning
roared at the rain
we were worshipping from
the safety of the porch
as she sambaed down the driveway
to the drumming of thunder.
The split wood is consumed
by flames but the dancer remains,
whirling barefoot in a giddy pirouette
delirious magical soaking wet.

23. *A Friend at Chase*

The hidden camera at the bank
records my inelegant contortions
terpsichorean agonies over
the figures posted in my account
a kneebend registers low teens
midsection follows
with a downward lurch
the vast benumbed head shakes
slowly back and forth
a dazed pendulum of denial
the lips are easily read: one word
repeated like a mantra
No, no, no, no.

My favorite teller still flashes
her thousand-dollar smile
unfazed by the shambles
of my finances could I charm her
into minor embezzlement
on my behalf move a couple of thou
into my account just until
the end of the month?
but Chase has taken over Chemical
and their hawkeyed accountants
inflexible as Edward G.
in *Double Indemnity*
would track us down
pregnant and broke in some
motel outside Baltimore
mugshots flashed on
America's Most Wanted
our moment of glory a two-minute
segment on tabloid news
and gone into the haze of
post-scandal afterburn
buried alive with the other
one-act chronicles
of American life.

24. *California*

On the main street of 29 Palms
the signs said "Haircuts"
"Tattoos" and "Guns" everything
you need to be a tough marine
a killing machine I remember Kenward
Elmslie who looked nothing like
a marine reciting *girl machine*
at NYU that first city autumn
I stepped off the boat and
his lockstepping language
fit the beat of the streets
girl machine girl machine
who cares what it means
entranced by the gutty verbal
promise of it all drooling
over moon canal mornings
and orchid orchards back in the day
and the years stretch forward to
this high desert evening
girl machine marine machine
at this altitude meaning falters
as we pass the herb in a circular motion
acrobatic chunks of laughter
tumble through the air like
diamonds falling through glycerine
the jungle juice thickens my thoughts
into a jammy consistency
liquefying segments of chronic
hilarity delicious and insubstantial
as July watermelon
a group of giggling consumptives
in this sanitarium
at the top of the world
coughing our pink lungs up
with each mouthful
of laughter and smoke.

25. *Happy Hour*

Watching the broccoli
boil in chicken broth
I understand a watermelon
bellowing for the hose
the soothing cascade of water
into a metal bucket
uncoils my insides
somebody says "now is the hour"
light runs in golden streams
across the flowered tablecloth
light enough for all
the rooms in my head.

The End

A catbird speaks to me
from a branch he owns
we are both surrounded by
thousands of lives and cars
and houses and their tragic
contents sad as a yard sale in
the early afternoon everything
somehow beyond repair
an immensity of puny striving
that will end up as nothing
but smoke I want to end as
something more tangible
than smoke and yet
to enter as ectoplasm
this marvelous blue air
to merge with light
to become like David Rattray
one of the invisible
weightless but golden
drifting with the cumulus
across continents
and centuries.

My epitaph will read:
died laughing badly behaved
but well remembered
If only my decease could be suspended
until I have transcended my dark roots
until the chakras burst from the spine
and the silken deposits leak out
like latex from a rubber tree
until I've opened the tear ducts the
bile ducts all the delicate faucets
and glands in the service
of a feathery sequence of verbals
that will pour like liquid bliss into
the clean pink instrument of your ear
Until then.

ABOUT THE AUTHOR

Max Blagg was born in the English Midlands in 1948. The youngest of twelve children, he declined a career in plumbing to pursue the literary life. He arrived in New York City in 1971 and has no plans to leave anytime soon.

ABOUT THE PHOTOGRAPHER

Ralph Gibson was born in 1939 and grew up in Hollywood. The son of an assistant director, he entered the Navy at age seventeen and was told there was an opening in photography school; he has occupied it ever since. He is an officer of the Ordre des Arts et des Lettres, holds honorary doctorates from the University of Maryland and Ohio Wesleyan, and is a Guggenheim fellow.

Portrait by Kristin Capp.

PINK INSTRUMENT

was set in Bembo, a typeface based on the types used by Venetian scholar-publisher Aldus Manutius in the printing of *De Aetna,* written by Pietro Bembo and published in 1495. The original characters were cut in 1490 by Francesco Griffo, who at Aldus's request later cut the first italic types. Originally adapted by the English Monotype Company, Bembo is one of the most elegant, readable, and widely used of all book faces.

Text design by Mark Polizzotti